Tales

of the

Human

Condition

Millicent R. Ally

This is a Crown and Clover Book
Published in 2012 by Millicent R. Ally

All rights reserved.
Copyright © 2012 by Millicent R. Ally
Foreword Copyright © 2012 by Gregory J. Schwartz

Without limiting the rights under copyright reserved above, no part of this book may be reproduced, stored in, or introduced into retrieval system, or transmitted in any form, or by any means, electronic or mechanical, including photocopying, recording or otherwise, without the prior written permission of both the copyright owner and the above publisher of this book.

FIRST EDITION
Ally, Millicent
Tales of the Human Condition: poems--1st ed.

Foreword	vii
Introduction	ix
Life	**12**
About Life	13
Human	14
Fourteen	16
We, the People	18
Numb	20
Battleground	22
Reality Check	24
Peak	25
Sunday	26
Work of Art	27
Judas	28
Masked Morality	30
An Informative Year	32
11.4.08	33
Ascension	35

Love — 36

About Love	37
Sentimental	39
Double Portrait	41
Chains of the Master	43
Peter Pan	45
Unworthy	47
Love Birds	49
Quest	51
Under Water	52
Back and Forward	54
Turning Point	55
Criminal	56
Vacancy	58
Bird of Prey	60
World's End	61

Introspection   64

About Introspection   65

The Profession   66

The Architect of Happiness   67

Be   68

The Great Wall   69

Warped   70

High School Blues   71

Apology   72

The Encounter   73

Fatal Flaw   75

Glory   76

The Future is Now   78

Secret Dawn   79

The Lifelong Process   80

A Death   81

God   82

About God   83

Basic Instruction	85
Purpose	86
Above	88
Misunderstood	89
Au Revoir	90
The Omega and the Alpha	91
Lazarus	93
Inhale, Exhale	94
Hide and Seek	95
The Distant Beyond	96
The Light	97
Epiphany	98
Immortal	99
Eternal Hymn	100
Conclusion	**102**
Acknowledgements	**105**
Biography	**107**

Foreword

Poetry is a fickle mistress, and the gifted, yearning artist its only suitor. Never conventional or predictable, a good poem has the power to elucidate the essence of the human experience with only a few words. It can soothe like a plate of mom's home cooking or plant a seed that cultivates a restful soul.

The written word proffers truths that can disturb, injure, uplift, and sanctify. Millicent Ally, the creator of the poems herein, is the purveyor of these truths. In a pop culture where inchoate creative icons are often just a voice-box for the genius, passion, and wisdom of an unnamed proxy, Millicent speaks with her own voice, drawn from a pool of experience that is disrobed and elucidated by her words.

Though she is a wildflower at heart, Miss Ally's work has the broad appeal of a classic red rose. Her voice is too travailed to blossom as a pure white rose and too meaningful for the ascribed neutrality of a yellow rose. Only the deep red rose fits the passion, pain, beauty, and richness of her writing.

Good poetry is ephemeral in its grandeur, much like a flower. Its effect rises and blooms on the reader's palate then fades amidst the hubbub and distraction of daily life. But each season in life provides the circumstances for the words of a good poem to again take root and blossom into fresh meanings and new interpretations--giving it new life.

Millicent's poems have this power, this dynamism, and this eternality. I invite you to breathe them in, savor them, and let them reside in your mind and heart. Nourished by your own joy, pain, and intellect, there they will blossom into a garden which will heal, assuage, and beautify the inner landscape of your soul.

It was Mark Twain who said, "If I had more time, I would have written less." On that sage advice, my words will now end so that Millicent's can begin…

Gregory J. Schwartz
Professor of Geography, Los Angeles Mission College,
author, *Five Ways to Save the Planet (in your spare time)*

Introduction

Tales of the Human Condition is my interpretation of this earthly animation. In the four sections I categorize as Life, Love, Introspection, and God, I aim to create a continuous whole that paints a picture of the multidimensional facets of a private journey. Over and over, I have found that Life, Love, Introspection, and God are crisscrossed, intertwined, intersected, and overlapped, helping me analyze my experiences, leading me down new paths, and sometimes offering me profound revelations. But, always, they inspire me to growth.

In this colorful collage of creativity, I reveal the ways in which each person, situation, and environment I've encountered has shaped my ideas of the world and the meaning of my presence in it. Through my experiences, I have come to realize I am more than my body, my gender, or my race. I am a spiritual entity who has chosen to take form. This form allows me to share my essence with others, to taste, to touch, to see, and to feel the substantial diversity of emotions this physical form offers.

Certainly, in pursuit of Life, I, like many of us, have not always chosen wisely. I have sought understanding about this world and asked, "Why?" confused by my own challenges. I have felt pain as well as happiness, anger as well as Love. I reflect with honor upon the person I was, the changes I have made, and who I have become by choice. It is with great joy that I am able to share all of this in

Tales of the Human Condition. Truly, Life is what one makes of it--it is a monumental opportunity. It is good to be alive! So make the most of it, and enjoy!

It is not the destination but the journey, step by step paving the way of destiny. The value in each and every moment--with an uncanny ability to comprehend the positive impact of that which is offered--is key. The collection of experiences forms a tapestry, woven together, creating a life.

Life

About Life

Life is an inexplicable journey. A compendium of variety and varying states of awareness, existence is both a personal matter and one which encompasses the entirety of mankind. In Life's grip, we each experience love and loss, joy and sorrow, success and failure--and, ultimately, death. These commonalities connect us one to the other despite our apparent differences. They create a mutual human bond.

It is our perceptions of these external forces which actually mold and reinforce reality to our betterment or detriment. In truth, this three-dimensional world is an illusion created to prod us forward to spiritual growth and evolution. If each situation and relationship is completely understood and its lesson learned, that is evidence of the grace of God. If we do not heed our lessons, we suffer.

This is Life.

Human

LOST

FOUND

STARTING
OVER

DEATH
GIVES
WAY

TO
BIRTH

REBORN
IN
FLESH

NEW SKIN

INFANT
AGAIN

CRAWL

WALK
STUMBLE
FALL

SCREAM

CRY

NOT
UNDERSTANDING
LIFE
AT
ALL

BEGIN
AGAIN

CYCLES
CHANGE

AND
SOME
REMAIN
THE
SAME

IN
THE
WORLD

I
KNOW

Fourteen

My name is Millicent Rachel Ally. I am a member of the human race. I observe and participate in this life, finding it a cold, cruel world, but it is the world as I was born into it.

I ponder this question, and it is how I find myself:
Who am I? I am a young woman in a male-dominated world, but I plan to demolish that thought.

Who am I? I am a member of a world where money talks and bullshit walks.
Who am I? I am a woman with just one life--such a short time to cram education, knowledge, wisdom, and all the essential tools for success into my brain and make them pay off before time and death take their toll on me physically.

Who am I? I am a person who walks along a lonely road, a person who will open many doors--searching, looking, hoping to find that Utopia that makes life worth living, envisioning that tangible-but-intangible Great American Dream.

Who am I? I have not yet fully discovered myself, but I keep myself from the pitfalls that pull so many others out of the race.
Who am I? I am not sure, but each day I live I am that much closer to knowing.

I have learned there are some questions one may never be able to completely answer. But still, I ask myself in the silence and the quiet of the night, who am I, who am I, who am I?

We, the People

Afflicted, I am, with tears, as the pain of
many injustices and inequities are perpetuated.
The mass majority is disconnected from God.
They sleepwalk through this non-reality reality.
The undeserving ascend, achieve fame, acclaim,
backed by money, power, and family names, in a
bestial society for the entire world to perceive the truth
wrapped in lies, cannibals feeding on each other's misery.
Life is a stage where the vindictive rogue becomes the hero,
while the pauper becomes rich in soul.

As we move counter-clockwise, counter-productive,
to regress in our attempts to regain our innocence lost.
'Tis all folly, and we the fools, ourselves begotten.
Time waits for no one, marching on past the blind,
while we, over-stimulated, become numb and desensitized
listening to the rants and ravings of a mad man saying,
"No child will be left behind," when we all have been left
behind, all forgotten, the consequences of which we can not
begin to imagine.

We, the Individuals, will pay. Yet We, the Individuals, no
longer matter. Did We ever? Us Pawns of Supply and Demand?
The Interchangeable Commodities of Big Business, getting
bigger? Bigger and more valuable than We, the People?
But, it was meant to be about Us, by Us, for Us.
From civilization to barbarism, devouring Our young,

They are left with no comprehension of history
or Themselves, just a fast food, fast loving, fast
living society, getting fat, and going nowhere fast:
Gen X, Gen Y, Gen I, Gen Me, Gen Now.

My mind races with thoughts of Them;
then a whisper of silence envelops
the world crashing into me.

Numb

I see you with sorrow.
I once believed characters like you existed only in jest,
fairy tales, and lies. My ignorance helped to abet you in
your self-inflicted crimes, then Life forced me to open my
eyes. I view you and wonder, "How is it possible to lose
thyself?"

You have been sadly misinformed.
You belong to yourself and can't run.
Do my ears deceive? I hear you are unable to find yourself,
although you have never examined yourself.
You must acquaint yourself with yourself.
You will then be better equipped to acquiesce to the
question, "Who am I?"

I know it is difficult. None of us wants the amusement to
end. Do you comprehend, in order to accomplish this task,
first you must like yourself? I realize you are not well, for
neither do you know, nor love, yourself. This disorder
devours souls, but onward on your quest you go.

Indeed you exploit your anatomy to numb the pain:
search for God in drugs, mistake sex for love,
and relinquish yourself from any of the blame.

I ask, "How do you exist?"
Please throw your excuses out the door.
There is no need to name names.

You are indeed the miscreant,
who squandered yourself away.

Battleground

I rage upon this world in which I live,
not with anger but with all the good I have to give.
I rage upon this world, knowing it cannot consume me,
not any of the things created in the illusions of this reality.

I rage upon this world for sanctity.
I pray so I never have to fight.
I will not give up doing what I believe is right.
I rage upon this world from dawn until night.

I rage upon this world staying positive,
affirming love is the best offering of mankind.
I rage upon this world and scream, "Wake UP."
Would you have me do anything less?
I rage upon this world with my best.

I rage upon this world so I may soar
to the ultimate heights of understanding.
I rage upon this world in search of truth and honesty.
I rage upon this world knowing we are sisters and
brothers with one God, a Father and a Mother.

I rage upon this world proclaiming that life
does not just go wrong. Do not cast the first arrow,
and no one will throw a stone.
I rage upon this world, not enraged but with
my zeal for life intact and engaged.
I rage upon this world with my words the only weapons I wield.

I rage upon this world until my purpose is fulfilled.
Then my spirit will move on, its energy transformed.

Reality Check

The fragility of a nearly finite life was close at hand.
It was death knocking on the door of a stranger
that shook me to the core,
and I pondered my own mortality.

Those who were vast in years surrounded me.
They spoke of their lives, of Life, and,
with wisdom, of their own impending deaths.

These elders told of friends who had gone before
and friends who were still fighting the good fight.
Yet, unanimous, their resounding voices,
as each one privately said to me, "I do not want to die."

This caused me to pause and reevaluate my life:
Was I living it to the fullest?
Many things on my agenda to accomplish,
and neither time nor place to bewail and blame.

Now, worry and grudges are curtailed, and my bag is light.
A fondness emerges for everyone who has crossed my trail,
merely for the exchange of perspectives.
I am a totality of forgiveness and love,
taking nothing in this Life for granted.

Peak

I ventured to paradise, inclined
to visit moments of madness. It
was a premeditated departure from my
reality, a vacation to reunite late nights
with a group of fast friends.
An adventure not soon forgotten.

I vowed to peak to the heights of ecstasy,
reign as an emancipated slave in a place
where I could violate commandments in
the presence of the watchful eyes of strangers.

In a binge-induced state, I shed no tears
for the suicide of my morality.
(It was neither nor never near to my heart.)
I existed in the nonexistence of rules,
 an exhausting place of irrational measure.

An explosive burst with a non-climatic
end, poised to relive and experience it all again.

Sunday

We conversed about me being inspired from above.
Yes, it is true, but I am also moved by lust and love,
the carnal desires of the flesh,
the pleasures of this body's experience.
Happily, I invited him in.
He politely peeled away the layers, having foreplay with
my mind. He was possessed of himself, always in control,
even in my midst. A mental shield covered the passion,
submerged, bubbling underneath the surface.
It was my freedom he yearned for, so I allowed him to kiss
it. From my freedom he rose; it dripped from his lips.
Through my garden he plundered, leaving me with a
new-found feeling of wonder.
My match perhaps, he knew the art of tantalizing the
thoughts; an astute discerner, he had a gift to view, deeply.
Our association was more than I believed it would be,
a day full of ease, enjoying each other's company,
no care for where any of it would lead.

Work of Art

Youth's death of frivolity liberates wisdom from the womb of its gestation. In hindsight, the view is always 20/20; evident are the lessons of a sublime orchestration. The past becomes a guide which helps us recognize our saving graces.

Our earthly saints, those who teach us, whether we determine the interactions are pleasant or not. That which is difficult is most important to heed, and in the gentle, loving acceptance of all that has transpired, we are sculpted into handsome reflections of the most high.

Judas

You are false as a friend.
You are false in your actions.
You are knowingly false and praise yourself as a prophet
to no end. I acknowledge this to myself with hesitant
reluctance, for once I held you on a pedestal, above all others,
in the highest regard. But the illusion that is you has
crumbled, and with the utmost certainty I can say,
you are a fraud.
From your lips come spiritual metaphors
crammed with vicious intent.
You assault and degrade with God's very principles,
using words to attack and attack, trampling those
who do not succumb to your narcissistic will.
You are self-important, self-righteous, and above your own
reproach, while neither a participant in the trials of, nor
responsible for, your fellow man, him whom you so
solemnly attest to be in service of.
All others are but commoners, as perceived from your lofty
perch, not deserving of even the most basic of courtesies.
I did not want to concede, though the signs were evident;
I can do nothing else but see with my singular eye, that
which I had previously ignored by denying its intuition.
From the depths of my being, in calm observation,
you are a carefully constructed image, created to deceive,
no more than a copy of those you admire, whose skin
you've arranged to hide the contrived arrogance of your
failing ego which is unraveling even as it clings to its
tower of superiority.

Yes, you are blessed with gifts which you currently misappropriate. Surely, you are well-studied in the spiritual and the upright. Of course, you are surrounded by prevailing light. Yet, still you venture towards the darkness, falling, solidifying your mere mortal state. And, understandably, I grieve for you. I shed wild tears. For in my heart, brother, I remember the way you were, and love you still.

Masked Morality

Impostors parade in broad daylight,
pretending to be what they are not,
portraying abstract, idealized characters,
saying whatever is necessary to fraud and sham.

But unable to behave continually in character,
their costumes, slowly unraveling, reveal,
to the keen observer, glimpses of the bone
beneath their deceits.

The masqueraders, caught unclothed, lash out,
denying any wrong-doing, claiming for themselves
a new role. In an instant, they become
the victims of extenuating circumstance,
void of responsibility.

And you, who discovered their facade, are cast as
the scoundrel in the drama, for seeing through it,
for demanding that the disguised ones
don a cloak of accountability.

How dare the rest of us require truth, honestly
and common humanity? Is not life challenging
enough without those in our sanctum ascribing
to betrayal? Conspiring against us?

Their cross is not mine to bear, only witness, therefore I bless them. Keeping my own mind focused and upright, I arrive at the only conclusion I can: I must forgive them as I want to be forgiven, because, in truth, they understand not what they do.

An Informative Year

There is a magic splendor in the unraveling of Life,
its grasp being beyond our control.

In the bitter-sweet surrender of allowing circumstances
to unfold lies the opportunity for miracles to occur.

When the only recourse to tragedy is laughter, it is a
profound testament to the resilience of the human soul.

The best devised plans are muddled by a chaotic world's
demands, but, in turning, fortunes may have a serendipitous
end.

The unexpected makes Life fortuitous, the unknown offering,
the potential to be talented, gifted not premeditated by
destiny.

Through the trials, and challenges overturned, an undiminished
spirit yearns to accomplish what it has heard "cannot be done."

11.4.08

I celebrate vivacity, commemorating the atonement of a lamented antiquity and the reconciliation of a land finally inclusive of its entire populace. Ataraxy has come. The expiation of America has commenced as we embrace our humanity, reclaiming every man's benevolence. A moment in time, signified by the accretion of the absinthe dreams of our forefathers, downtrodden, beaten, but spirits never broken. We ascend on the backs and shoulders of their sacrifices, confronting our conscience as we amend history, put the past to rest, and bless our collective manifest destiny. My emotions overwhelm and conveying their sentiments conflicts, but they are verily poignant. I say, with an ecclesiastic heart, that a man spoke to me and to a nation. From his words a movement, unparalleled in five decades, was born. I, like the many, have been infused with a new fidelity in the possibility of the impossible. It is the revelation of a new age. The tangible red, white, and blue American Dream. I am bubbling, bursting, and exploding with joy; brimming with pomp and pride; always hoping but never truly thinking, as a little black girl, that I would ever see this day. Then I hear the words, and in elated disbelief, I cry; I cry purging tears as blue as the ocean is wide, for those who have given their lives and died. I am a witness to the expression of dual generations that saw beyond color and chose to view the intellect and character as a measure to form an opinion of a man. I appreciate you, Mr. President, for having the audacity to believe we could truly overcome the tragedies and flawed policies of a never-quite fulfilled constitutional legacy. No matter the complications of the tasks, I thank you. I thank you, Mr. President, for being a man beyond reproach. Now, I no longer feel like a motherless child. Indeed, because of you, I can claim this country of the United States of America as mine, too.

Ascension

The Past is history.
Uncertainty is the Certain Mystery.
Within the Mystery unfolds
tremendous untold Possibilities.
For the Unknown is our Friend,
having no Beginning,
having no End.

Love

About Love

Love is the basis of life and creation, the foundation of man and the universe. It is the truth hidden in each individual. It is the eternal flame of the human spirit, rising throughout the ages.

Love is varied, evocable in every relationship: between father and child; husband and wife; sisters, brothers, friends, lovers, and, most importantly, within one's self. The ability to love, to give and to receive, is innate to every human being, but it must be nurtured, otherwise this capacity dulls over time.

But it is romantic love that instills the greatest passion--and the greatest confusion. Romantic love is the meeting of two minds, two hearts, and two souls. It can bring a sense of wonderment. In its most rarefied form, romantic love brings utter happiness, complete acceptance, and a heart full of joy.

Unfortunately, romantic love is often engaged simply to fulfill the ego, and leaves in its wake disappointment and emptiness. It is only when we love unconditionally that the dynamic of the relationship is felt in its purest expression.

In my experience, I have found romantic love to be an operation of trial and error. More times than not, the person I believed I loved was either just a reflection of an aspect of myself or a manifestation of the lack of love I had for myself. However, I have discovered that each relationship--and its subsequent loss--clarifies what I desire in a mate, and thus, fine-tunes my direction and encourages me on my journey.

As I become more loving and gentle with myself, I discover a deeper meaning of Love. Love starts in the temple of my corporeal residence and emanates from there, without hesitation, to all who cross my path. If I love myself, I am loved, and the search for Love is over.

Sentimental

If they ask, I will tell them I loved you.
When I loved you.
Why I loved you.
Where I loved you.
How I loved you.
Who I was when I loved you.

I will leave no detail to chance.
I will leave nothing to their vivid imaginations.
It will all be readily explained.
I will share our epic and title it.
I will give it its proper name.

If they ask, I will tell them how I am, having loved you.
Am I different?
Better?
Am I the same?

Did I learn?
Did I lose?
Did I grow?

Is the fondness I felt more evident as I reflect?
As time goes by?
Or do I have regrets that flutter in my mind?

Is it possible to feel again as I did then?
Or, having loved and lost, has the possibility come to an end? So many questions, yet I have only one reply: Yes, once, I most definitely loved you.

Double Portrait

Portraits of you and me fornicating embellish my mind.
I awaken, and I wonder how it all began.

In each still an emotion lies frozen in a frame,
flashbacks which are timeless.

These pictures represent all that I have become, what
I never thought I could be, a consequence of your ruing.

These are my relics, my capsules in time to where it all
began. No, it was not all of your doing, but somehow in
the battle we waged you won the war.

I pleaded, please take only my heart, but you would have
nothing less than my soul. I begged for mercy. I swore my
eternal loyalty to you, but you would hear nothing of it.

You, once a serendipitous angel of delight and a trepidatious devil of deceit, how naïve of me to believe you could
ever love anything pure or clean.

A rebel who revels in the red light zone of harlots, tricks,
jacks, fiends, and whores, one night stands of pornographic
scenes behind closed doors.

Stalls, rooms, bars, saloons, anywhere your salacious mind
voyages, soon after your physical body must explore, laying
down all your rules for any who dare play your game.

Never deceitful, always deceitful, your thievery; quick with hearts and souls, how loudly you proclaim so-called words of truth and honesty, but a villain you are, just the same.

My awakening, and all that is left is an empty capsule yearning to retrieve my heart, so I may love again. Longing for my soul, so I may have peace.

Wanting to regress so I may be what I once longed not to be. Left with only hallucinations and dreams of things, before this too late awakening.

Chains of the Master

I helped to build his fortress.
Gave him dominion over my tenure.
Made this man my master.
Yet he guards himself against me.

This immense betrayal, I combat with silent outrage.
The lies he hides are housed in me.
His paranoia evidenced in their disclosure.
I have become, despite my loyalty, an evildoer.

Although I am not the culprit who castrated his heart,
still, he trespasses while I trespass not,
but wonder about the crimes committed
that fuel his cruelty.

I view him from a cell,
a barred prison formulated in my mind.
For I am an emancipated slave who has
refused to leave the service of my lord,
as long as he beckons.

I desire above all else his affection,
for him to appease my yearning,
to have his loin dagger
penetrate my temple.

I, indeed long to touch his core,
to wrap my soul around his own,
and perhaps discover our innocence lost.

But the armor he wears thwarts all attempts.
I, an addict, became accustomed to chasing his love.
I enabled him to violate my body and usurp my mind.
I am at last corrupted. He was the death of my humanity.

Peter Pan

He strolled back into my life.

I was uncertain why the universe had sent him.
I had utterly abandoned my emotions concerning our relationship. I had resigned not to care about any masculine counterpart, for now. I belonged to myself and had no one else to consider. It was my time to be selfish.

In this particular moment, that's how I wanted my life to unfold.

I was cautious of his presence.
Simultaneously, I welcomed him in.
I was put off by emotions that might distract me.
My heart was full of love for myself.
I had no room for any others.

It was not to be our destiny this time, nor had it been previously.

Still, I liked the twinkle in his eyes.
I enjoyed his hands lusting over and after me.
He wanted to be my provider.
He wanted to protect and keep me from harm's way.
But he had not the means to sustain me, and he did not have the courage to try.

He could no longer hold my affections.

He had once caused me great pain.
But he would not again, for I had changed.
The girl who had been enthralled by him
had become a woman.
Now, that woman recognized him with the clarity
of new eyes.
He was Peter Pan, the boy who never grew to become a man.

Unworthy

Voluntarily, I lie beside the source of my sorrow.
I wake from another restless night; my body is still,
but my mind broods over scenes of fornucopia.
The scent of sex permeates the air; its taste lingers
upon my lips.

The splendor that was has gone, enveloped by the dawn.
My suitor has become a stranger, and I a devotee
he concluded was damaged goods,
unworthy of his intimacy.

Before his judgment was passed,
he conspired--with my assistance--
against me, and led me into the lonely
land of lovers alone.

I became his hostage, engaging in this deceptive amusement.
It was a dangerous liaison, but I played along.
I kissed lips whose kisses I might not posses,
perceived the emptiness of vacant eyes focusing on me,
and all these things I pretended not to notice.

I co-founded this universe,
but it is greatly to my disliking.
He partook, not taking.
I gave him the un-given which he scorned.

I walked through this portal with myself.
I stagger from this debasement
with barely my virtue left,
sullen tears in my eyes.

With these words I confess,
he was my fire, a rascal and a liar.
All I wished for and more I had not.

Love Birds

This relationship in which I asked of your participation
demanded of you illegal lengths of fortitude.
Yet we forged ahead, you, with cooperative opposition,
me, with a cloudy plan.

I presented myself and situation honestly.
I burst upon your world with the chaos of mine in hand.
I exhibited for your conjecture all the facets of my
dysfunction, confident you would understand the
errors in your own nature.

But while you waged war with your emotions,
unwilling to concede,
my persistence eroded your barriers,
and, with uncertainty, you welcomed me into your domain.

Our dispositions were not the same,
but we enjoyed playing the other's game
and never tired of the other's company
(although, on occasion, we did adjourn to linger,
momentarily, in each other's absence).

But those separations drew us back, and frantic,
both of us concluding it had been too long
(even when our prior visit had been
only the night before).

What madness reigned? I wonder how
I could not have realized that what
we had labeled Love was only sickness,
the fever of obsession.

Quest

Unable to disregard my thoughts of our professional
acquaintance and the amorous current which ran between us,
I go in search of you . . .

Fixated on the memory of the charge your presence gave
me, the way your charismatic spirit magnetized my own,
I go in search of you . . .

Not satisfied with the words at my disposal,
unable to express your brilliance and
how strongly I still feel, I go in search of you . . .

I capture people, places, and situations in life,
recreate feelings and the intimacy of moments in my most
private intellect, and then I go in search of you . . .

From my hand-crafted golden memories, I create fantasies
about our encounter, which nonetheless fade as time passes,
therefore, I go in search of you . . .

Perhaps the universe will sanction our connection
and lead us to meet again, lending to our attraction
the legitimacy which it deserves.
Until then, I go in search of you . . .

. . . the revised destination on my itinerary.

Under Water

He pursued me, this boy who represented himself as a man.
He whispered to me under cover of the night, as our naked bodies converged.
He flowed beneath my skin, seeped into every pore.
He became my all, the very air I breathed.

His kisses, his touch, his very being I believed.
It felt like love, but I was, instead, mistaken.
Once this man--no, boy--comprehended the disposition of my heart, he released all responsibility and vanished.

Left alone, in shambles, I retreated, heard his echoing words: "I could spend the rest of my life with you."
"I am yours as long as you will have me."
"I am yours"; "I am yours"; "I am yours."

So spoke my torment, my torture,
as I shed tears at the shame, the betrayal,
the time I'd spent, the time I'd lost,
and sank into the ocean of my own despair.

The weight of sorrow I imagined to be more than I could bear, but it was not. I survived, becoming stronger for the lessons I had learned.
The love that ran so deep does not exist,
and the woman who loved the boy is no longer.

I have seen him since, made polite conversation,
but he is a ghost, a mirage, a stranger to my eyes.
For with selfishness and disregard, he devastated me.
Yet, I am here, standing still, as the woman who,
survived loving him.

Back and Forward

I flee from the love I have for him,
which has followed me through years
and possibly life times.

Endless is my love for him,
although it has become an obstacle
in my way.

My spirit longed to settle our karmic debts,
extricate itself from the past
and its devouring pain.

I love him, but am tired of bearing him;
he has become a burden,
a stumbling block.

We progress, regress; this back and forth must end.
I have no more time to waste desiring him
nor in denying my love for him.

Our so-called "friendship" now wrecked,
I assess the damage, with conflicted understanding,
 finding no comfort in my loss,
I cry--and utter a tacit goodbye.

Turning Point

I dutifully entrusted the decision to my heart, but my heart had surrendered. My spirit's soul sent out an S. O. S., pleading for me to reclaim my stronghold. I heard him speak of love when his actions belied it. Either he desired me at every moment or cast me off for drink and fellow foolishness. Then wrecked and ravaged he would return, appealing for the comfort of my bosom. My arms opened wide, I would welcome him.

Why? I loved him--although we both knew I deserved better.

Neither happy with him or without him, at the pinnacle of my dilemma my intellect instructed me to act. Survival became my priority; I could not afford to lose my optimism, nor would I wait for him to realize the depth and sincerity of my heart. Though I aided in the creation of this affliction, I released him without hesitation, not bound by fear, alert to the Love I must have for myself in order for another to consider me dear.

Criminal

He was a brute by all accounts,
but a Romeo in the same vein.

The complexity of his character
made me ponder him again.

He was treacherous,
but hid a kind heart in the depths of his soul.

A law unto himself.
One of a kind.

No others.
There was no mold.

No logic to the things he did.
He had a conscience he could reason with;

Survival was the key to his master plan;
money was the outcome, a means to an end.

I watched him from afar,
until I asked him to come hither and tell.

Mystified,
I was unable to suppress my desire.

I longed to possess and capture him, for he resided
in a world I could only imagine in my dreams.

I yearned to hold and keep him near,
but like a wild thing, he had to be free.

Vacancy

A face of armor he wore, a shield to mask himself,
to keep intruders out. Does he ever smile?
I wondered, perplexed, and yet intrigued.
From a distance, I watched,
until the day he spoke to me.

He viewed myself and others typically with the same
blank gaze. He spoke, at times, with reverence,
but it too would disappear, into the flat affect
of his ordinary monotone.
The words he used were soft and subtle,
urging you to draw near: "Come closer and listen."

Listen in ignorance, you did, transfixed
by the calm of his voice, which politely
slapped your face, dismissing your presence,
as if you were no more than a servant.
Then he'd stare, unaffected by the situation,
leaving you bewildered. Did he have an evil twin?

The assurance of money he rested upon.
Insufficient passion for life was the battlefield
his spirit warred upon, an explanation of the
sadness in his eyes. A soul in flesh, but his world
was built of glass, therefore he guarded his reality
afraid he might be transported back to his wonder years,
shattering the fears erected on the ego.

My observation after studying him:
Some have nothing so they learn how to give.
Others have everything, and still can't find a reason to live.

Bird of Prey

He was my suitor.
He called upon me,
sought my company
with deep adoration.

Somehow his eyes changed.
No longer did he gaze upon me with the same kindness.
I had become a stranger in his view.
Our warm connection had been mysteriously cooled.

An avalanche of emotions welled up from my depths.
I noticed floating a poisonous cloud, composed
entirely of the treacherous lies
of a plotting, waiting, black-winged vulture.

She scrounged and fed on the remains of our relation,
eagerly destroying what had been
and fed it to him, chased with all his insecurities,
until his gullet was full.

Relishing the revelation of her fallacies,
he believed I had been too good to be true.
Satisfied with her carrion,
he steered clear of our love and his heart withdrew.

I was left in a state of disbelief.
I mourned our passing.
I cried, and with my tears I put it all to rest.

World's End

The evidence of his parents' indulgence,
confident and casually assured was he.
Selfish, spoiled, and quietly arrogant,
he existed only to please himself.
He camouflaged his background
with the meager appearance he chose,
wearing it as if it belonged to him,
this façade meant to keep groundlings away.

Drawn to his beauty and charisma,
I entered his world with no invitation,
believing myself the predator, ready to prey upon
his amazing energy, which emerged from a foreign
source unlike anyone I had ever envisioned.

He took me from tranquility to rage,
where he resided, simultaneously,
alive at both ends of the spectrum,
a wild expression of extremes,
the very definition of internalized chaos,
a live example of the destructive nature of those
who devalue their lack of limitation,
the culmination of an undisciplined spirit
bound by a physical shell.

He, unable to grasp the relentlessness of
his pursuit of self-persecution,
was vexed by my attempts to calm his anguish;

he desperately believed in his rage
and his dwelling inside it,
and soon I discovered my love could not soothe him,
a discovery which ruined me.
Seeds of contempt grew out of my heart.

I was despondent, clutching at the remains of our bond.
In a final attempt, I descended upon his presence and spoke:
We cannot continue if you persist in this manner. You deploy cruelty and madness. You ask my heart to accept what is unacceptable. You attempt to convince me to go against my principles, and you ask me to be satisfied with your mere drippings. You must cease and desist. For, as definitely as I am a woman, I will revolt with all that I possess. My love will sour and you will desire its sweetness lost. You will miss the comfort of my arms and then it will be too late.

To my desperate plea,
with the mind of a man, he laughed.
And that was the end of us.

Introspection

About Introspection

Embarking on an introspective journey, void of the ego, is an arduous task--but necessary for one's self discovery. The self which I've set out to discover is that which resides at the center of any problem and every solution. By acknowledging my character flaws and accepting my own shortcomings with love, forgiveness, and a willingness to change, I improve in my humanity.

With each internal dialogue I undertake, I align myself with the source of my nature. It is only when I become still, withdraw my senses from the world and lend a deliberate ear to the divine that shines so brightly within that I find peace. Then, the illusions of the world, the notion that I am only flesh and bone, disappears, and I remember: I am a spiritual being experiencing a physical life.

I hear it said that wisdom arises from living life, but I have learned that great wisdom is gained through a deepening acquaintance with my inner self and the spirit that animates me. The sages teach us that our primary purposes are to inspire, to create, to be of service, and to love. Armed with the hard-won knowledge of my self, I can tap into limitless possibilities. With my self intact, I can become a vessel of brilliant light to illuminate the world.

The Profession

I am a storyteller.
I am a verbal stylist.
I am a linguistic expressionist.
I am an urgent philosopher,
highlighting, spotlighting,
and enticing you
with my perspective
on the human condition
and all its idiosyncrasies.

I splatter my intentions on the page,
display the beauty of thoughts and of emotions.
I capture the oddity of a single moment for you to see,
and give you permission, with my words,
to analyze your world and its juxtapositions
as through the eyes of a stranger.

Where you are afraid to venture,
I find adventure, and from there,
I may pose the complex questions;
perhaps make you think,
thereby, emancipating you,
opening up your mind,
becoming your mirror image.

I am a poet (do you see?).
But more than that,
I am a collector of life experience, data, and memories.

The Architect of Happiness

I tempt providence with my idealism and the expansiveness of my romantic heart. My personal gaiety is finally my priority, and selfishly I aim to please. My ego steps aside, out of my way.

I surmount life and am distinguished, regardless of my circumstances. This newfound disposition, its beauty and simplicity astounds me. The thoughts I choose linger, so I reside in them peaceably--and they in me.

Good is accessible ever present, despite the uncertainty of stability. I remain steadfast, not allowing my eyes to deceive. It is my imagination that has contented me, so, dutifully, I remain flexible.

Even through the duration of my isolation, my joy is devout. Moment by moment, I am emerging as the person I have imagined. I am satisfied with life as I live it, and yet I am eager for more. Therefore, I do not mind, nor tend to the passage of time.

All is well. I ready myself to receive the benevolence that is truly mine.

Be

I am exactly myself.
How can I be anyone else?
I don't wish to waste time
wondering why "he" or "she"
is like "this" or "that."
Wondering can only cause me
to wander from my path.

I urge you, too, to do the same:
exist within your own space.
We are all unique.
No need for us to be homogeneous.
Perhaps you misperceive me
as subtracting from your presence, here,
since I live unencumbered.

Excuse me. I beg your pardon.
Don't point your finger.
Your accusations will fall on deaf ears.
The "tried and true" is "false and failed."
The patterns of the old have become obsolete.

Catch up! There are many in the midst of spiritual awakening.
I bless you despite your erroneous assumptions.
I give you permission to be yourself,
by being undeniably me.

The Great Wall

The disguise I wear is no more eccentric than yours.
I cover my appearance to defend my borders.
I am afraid you might see my imperfections and failings.
My supreme desire is your nonjudgmental acceptance.

Still, my insecurities prevent your coming near.
It is only my ego shouting loudly of past failures;
it announces every doubt in an attempt
to drown out a quieter truth:

I am a divine expression of the universal mind.
I must express the best of myself,
though the cloak of my ego would have me shelter in.
I must allow my benevolent light to shine.

This is the key to my inevitable victory.

Warped

I lived my life fast and hard, while pretending not to notice.
But now I choose to take ownership of this predicament,
to understand the numerous unanswered questions,
to analyze the detrimental choices I made, which
obscured both judgment and divine reason.
Void of closure, the very thought leaves me immediately numb.

I once adhered to an ever-changing situational morality
suggested by capricious moods.
It was a doctrine of madness, I yearned not to think.

But I must attempt to make sense of it,
my continual disillusionment with life.
I am suffocating in the choke-hold of this reality.
I crave to be a child again, absent of life's complexities,
if only for a moment, just to catch my breath.

What is left of me is bitter and cold.
I claim the blame, fashioning my shame,
accountable for my own depravity,
stating growing up did monstrous things
to this so-called human being.

High School Blues

A crime committed not of my own volition,
absurd that I feel guilty.

Alone. Loneliness. Is it my crime?
My isolation the fine?

Unable to post bail, I suffer more in this desolate hell,
in a cell which confines not my body, but my mind.

An emptiness, a black hole, sucks away my breath;
the anguish, a pillow of sharp thorns, provides no rest.

The eternal ticking of that damn clock reminds me time is
running out. Unable to escape, will I languish until I
perish? Until doomsday says I've failed?

Suddenly, I see a shaft of light, but turn away.
Do I want to stay? In this hell-haven? To pity myself?

To have an irreproachable reason to blame all the rest for
the creation of my confinement in this abyss?

Mortified by my weakness, I realize the nightmare of alienation
astride my mind. Loneliness, perhaps a God-given friend?
But it feels like a punishment for some heinous sin.
Ashes to ashes, dust to dust. Birth as one . . .

. . . die alone you must.

Apology

Regardless of the lack of intercourse and the inconsistency of our relationship, I must announce that I love you, Mother.

My love for you reigns paramount, despite the absurdities of our past, which bind us in a pedigree of dysfunction.

Neither you nor I are to blame for the mishaps of our ancestors. The past is beyond both you and me.

I can reflect on the choices made by our family and its parental predecessors with empathy. I avow, the cycle must be broken.

Thus, I hold none accountable, unless I hold myself accountable. Do you do the same, Mother?

Nothing less than children of God, learning from our choices. Forgiveness is the only way to free ourselves from emotional, familial, bondage.

Fallen from grace, we have, if we are unwilling to release the past and move ahead. So, Mother, let us forgive, and forget.

If we do not, it will be our life's greatest regret.

The Encounter

He was a mutation, a shape shifter,
not bothered or tied to conventional morality.
A contradiction within a contradiction.
A brute by nature with the capacity to be humane.

He was extraordinary.
The epitome of style and elite taste.
He detested anything common,
would grieve for his own death if ever he discovered
himself to be ordinary.

There are those who consider him a monster.
His tolerance was slow and few, in his opinion,
capable of ascending to his lofty plateau.
I was bewitched by a soul who believed himself less
tortured, because he acted upon all of his impulses.
I scoffed, "It is merely your insatiable libido which
navigates you. I advise you to examine interiorly the
source of your impulses; do not act unless you constantly
intend to live your life with regrets."

It was strange, though. He spoke of no regrets, only boxes.
A room full of boxes.
The facility he visited in his psyche, stored the wages of his
sins. The place he objectified his actions, rationalized his
deeds.

He tantalized me,
an enigma I was unable to wholly understand.
There was something beautiful to his calculated
carelessness.

The lust in his eyes devoured me,
lips kissed with such illicit passion,
as he explored the orifices of my body.
My curiosity sent shock waves of desire through me.
I surrendered, against my better judgment,
in blatant disregard of everything I knew,
and I lay with him.

Fatal Flaw

I see the darkness in your eyes,
yet it is of no comfort to me
to peek through your disguise.
Rather, I envy your control.
As you effortlessly cast me aside,
I wish I could crawl inside,
steal your life, and be other than I am.
No longer a woman, I would become a man,
fight against my nature, hold the gun,
with you at the other end;
look through the windows of your view,
breathe sharp and harsh as you do.
I gave you life, and I would take it from you.
Peer through God's eyes and the devil's eyes, too.
Freeze time. Laugh at sin.
Be born again. Starting from this moment,
knowing more than I knew then.

Glory

I loved him because I could.
Like a cup, my heart overflowed
with love for those who had none,
or perhaps, not enough.
He tormented himself,
believing he had stolen my heart
to fill his vacant soul.

No! I gave it freely, for it was mine to give.
Nothing of mine can anyone steal.
What belongs to me comes as a gift given freely
by One greater than either he or I,
a present to be shared.

He had been empty (he would agree),
but his emptiness, and all that I learned from him,
filled me. And though I lost him whom I had loved,
from that great loss I gained myself.

I became strong, and my strength gave me joy.
Secure in the knowledge of who I am,
I grew in faith that what is good and honest prevails.
I am in the world but not of the world,
and the world does not define me.

He is not the first, nor will he be the last.
I shall laugh again, and again, shed a few tears.
Life encourages change, and change brings growth.

Growth opens the pathway to rebirth.
The bounty of the universe, yours to receive.
While most of us desire to be full,
others choose to be more or less empty.

The Future is Now

The elders profess, we are the future,
but the future ceases to exist when seen
from the present, which is the only constant--
a gift given us currently to birth the future into reality.
Those that herald the need for future planning
obscure the depth of the future's meaning.
We are the future; creating it everyday.
Our future is now, here,
and on display.

Secret Dawn

This splendor, its enormity, and past unfamiliarity
is non-consequential. The happiness which is, I possess.

Someone whispered to me the secret.
A flash, a turning point,
and all that existed disappeared.
I dropped through the rabbit hole,
where questions that had plagued me
began to reveal themselves as answers
and quench the thirst of my desire
to comprehend the world I see
with more than the vision of a mortal
living in a three-dimensional reality.

I thought I had misplaced myself,
but my spirit sang a song,
leading and pushing me along.
"To partake in this
universe as a co-creator,
wisely choose your thoughts, today,
manifesting the world in which you play."
I proclaim this for any who hear and listen.
Some, to this principle, say,
"Show me so I can believe."
I practiced my desired dreams
and changed the life I lead.

The Lifelong Process

The outer appearance of things does not sustain,
nor does it suffice as nourishment for the soul.
Only when the world descends, does the trek begin.
The rest is but a waking dream.

The totality of everything of this world
means nothing once you discern its bewitchment.
Then, the temperamental human ego crashes,
and forgiveness and love are raised upon its throne.

This is what the prophets of the ages have told of:
not a distant heaven, far way, but a heaven here on earth.
The joy that resonates from inside one's self,
no man can take from you.

The task assigned to all of us is to stay in this awareness
every single day, despite the thieves who lie to us
with the perception of the senses. Thus, we extricate
ourselves from karma, and take the first steps along the
path of enlightenment.

A Death

I will be myself for a little while longer.
For now, I will continue to be the person
everyone has come to know.

But when it is expected of me least,
I will shed this familiar skin
and become someone no one had envisioned.

I will continue on my path,
altered, other than I had been.

Transformed before others' eyes,
I will pretend not to remember my metamorphosis,
as if I had always been this new creature.

The creature I appear to be now,
I will only preserve small relics locked safely away
of what had come before.

Phantasms of another that linger in the eclipse
between twilight and dawn,
ascending each day as if I had never gone.

God

About God

God is the source and creator of the universe, but since this description falls short of expressing God's true greatness, I set out to write the most perfect, most expansive explanation of God possible. This was a huge mistake! Under so much self-assigned pressure, I considered my ideas of God to the point of complete and utter frustration. Where to start? What to write?

Eventually, I realized, if I wrote from my heart, it would be enough, and if I left anything out, indeed, God would understand. Suddenly, I understood that whatever I write is perfect. Perfection exists in everything said and unsaid because all exists in God--the duality exists simultaneously with that which is complete, perfect, and whole.

So, with humility, I define God and what He/She means to me: God is the source and creator of the universe. Yes, God is all-encompassing, omnipresent wisdom and love, a Presence of such magnitude It often goes unrecognized. But God is also the wind that blows through our hair, the air we breathe. He/She is the effortless beating of each of our hearts. God is the mind which animates our personalities; the tree that gives us shade; the water which cleanses our bodies and quenches our thirst. God is every person, every sound, every creature, great and small.

Above all, God is our constant spiritual fortifier, replenishing us when we seek Him/Her with meditation, prayer, and quiet contemplation; centering and guiding us and making the most crooked of our roads straight.

Basic Instruction

The scions of the Father dream.
Night bleeds into another dayspring.

The uncertain moments of yesterday escape at dawn.
I wake gleefully as the regrets and bygones fade with the new good morn.

Transport not the past, for it does not live honestly.
Master your zeal, tending to it, paying forward the blessings of today.

This is your best, a testament to the simplest request for a beautiful earthly incarnation into flesh.

Purpose

I know You put me here to experience and feel.
I want to taste this earth's appeal.
What shall I ask You for? Riches?
Fortune? Fame? For the world to shout my name?

No, You reply. *These dreams are not profound.*
They are the desires of every man,
from then, to now.
Think before you demand.
This world is a flower blooming
right in the palm of your hand.
Now think: What does your heart require?

Happiness! That is my one true desire!
I ask for its essence, which I cannot touch.
Can I have it completely, if I am clever?
For all my days? In my youth and late tomorrows?
Will You allow me to devour happiness forever?

Then this lyric my heart sings,
Let her never be far from my plight,
for many are rich, but still can not acquire
the happiness they long for in quiet hours.

Happiness, she calls to me;
love, and what great fun that will be.
The two of us together, hand and hand.
Happiness and love in the grip of romance.

Indeed, that would be my dream come true.
I then would be the wealthiest man in all the land,
possessed of the rarest possession any alive can have.

Above

Turn to Me in your hour of need.
When you feel lost, I shall guide your spirit that searches;
I shall fill the heavens with stars and always light your way.

Turn to Me; there is no other.
I am your friend, your Father, Mother, Sister, Brother.
I will give unto you even in your darkest hour.

Turn to Me; there is no other.
I conceived you, grew you, gave you your first breath.
I am by your side even when your soul does not rest.

Turn to Me; there is no one greater.
So turn to Me and say My Name: G. O. D.
Goodness Over Divinity, for I will not forsake thee.
Turn to Me; turn to Me; turn to Me.

Misunderstood

I don't think I like this world anymore.
Birth, life, love and death.
What, exactly, is living for?
I've asked God, but have heard no reply.
Now my rage is killing the good I have inside.

Is nothing sacred?
Should I have hope?
I am losing faith.

In my dismay, I call my cousin Marc.
But he's not there.
His life was stolen,
taken in vain.

Now I shout out in anger:
WHY HAVE YOU TAKEN HIM?
Don't I deserve to know?
Have you forsaken us?
Father, do you not love Your children anymore?
And if so what is this Life for?

Au Revoir

With all the sadness of the world
flooding her innocent eyes,
a child asks, "Why do we have to die?"

Shocked by the innocent frankness
of the question from one so young,
I paused . . .

Well, we are spiritual beings from the great beyond.
We are eternal energy, the testament to God's undying love.
His love for us so great, He gave us physical form,
to be as He, able to dream and create.

Thus, from the non-physical we are born,
focusing our energy into the temporary shelter
of the body-suit we don. Then we have life experiences
which help us to gather information
for our souls' collective evolution.

And when the work of our life is done,
we return to the eternity of love,
the Home from which we have come.

The Omega and the Alpha

Overwhelmed by the emotional crash and burn,
languishing in the sorrow of the storm released
and overturned, raging at the past unearthed,
yearning after the love I chased, it was a multitude of
issues, long suppressed, which churned; streaming tears,
I howled with the aching of an abandoned child.

The gleam of sharp metal presented itself,
shiny and new, the blade I pressed to my flesh.
I cut, momentarily alleviating my distress.

Red liquid poured from me, and with a hand not of
my mind, I cut again slow and steady, a second time.
With each slice upon my flesh, I slipped further and
further from the weight with which I was fraught,
but it was a desperate assault.

I drifted in and out of rational thought, aware only
of the freedom promised by each stroke.
A solution, I thought, as I watched the magenta of life
coursing out of my vein.

As my time came terrifyingly near, from out of nowhere
Spirit said, "It is not over for you, you have too much to
share." And with shame in my breast,
I placed the call to rescue myself.

I found redemption in my hour of disgrace,
value in a life I was almost willing to cast away.

Lazarus

I entered into a solemn quarantine to awaken from my life-lived slumber. I proceeded into darkness to shut the bright world out. The stillness of the silence deafened me to all but the words whispered on the wind: "Nothing is ever lost, nor can anything outside one's self be found."

Inhale, Exhale

Peace descended.
The chaos stilled.
Reality receded.
The world withdrew.

Stillness and serenity reigned.
Calamity transformed to calm.
Actions told of only love.
Words of kindness resonated in the air.

My burdens were lifted
by the One who can carry the load.
And, as if from a long night of sleep,
the dreamer of my youth was restored.

Hide and Seek

Although you conspire in secret,
He knows the weight of your heart.
Each lie you hide, every word you misconstrue,
all the crimes you commit, the precise count of
all the dark deeds you perpetrate under the cover of night
will come to light.

You will not get far.
Everywhere you go,
there you are.

And He is with you, tied to you
as close as you are to yourself.
You may try to hide, only to find
your karma beside you, in front,
and catching you from behind.

The Distant Beyond

Spirit is the cradle from which we are born.
The source of our origin, obscure and unknown.
Incarnated into the physical, I tread across the ticking
minutes, but Father Time is not truly yours nor mine.
His sands slips through our hands and the hour glass
with the dissipation of a quiet storm, until we yield to
the paradoxical Omega to which we must return.

The Light

I pen my gratitude line by line, for much have You beloved
me. With this humble gesture, I thank You not only for
grace and courage, but also for the struggle and strife that
challenge my faith and remain steadfast. If it were not for
sorrow, its counterpart joy I could never know.
Without weakness, I could never comprehend strength.

In the acceptance of the lows, I can rejoice in the highs
and understand the balance You have imbued in the celestial
plan. Schooled in this knowledge, I bow to Your Will.
And if the trappings of this world have me acting in anger,
I will examine myself.

I'll ask not if You have forsaken me,
but will turn from my weakness,
exhume my gratitude, and
experience the universal good
You provide generously every day.

Epiphany

I peer from previously skeptical eyes,
redeemed and filled with wonder,
into the brilliant vibrance of the macrocosm
where I am reflected in every face I see,
without borders or cultural exceptions.

Erased is the distinction between
the "exterior" and "interior."
The steady thread of my awareness maintains
the constancy of my connection with the limitless whole.

With no beginning, without end, the pulse of joy flows
through life and, too, through death, and back again,
expressing the potentialities of God's eternal cycling energy,
His limitlessness, and the completeness He has created
diligently.

Immortal

Tears I shed no more for this life and its ubiquitous, continual passing. Death is but a changing of the guard. What pertinent reason is there to mourn infinity? While our temporary identities meet their demise, the gist of you and me blows across the winds of eternity.

It is ours, the opportunity to be born, but the edict of the natural universe dictates for every beginning there is an end. So once memories of this earthly experience have been gathered, assembled, and preserved in the sanctuary of the ethos, to the invisible from which we came, we all must return.

Eternal Hymn

The infinity of my existence is You. I belong to no other.
You are the source of my very being, my reason to live,
to view another dawn, to see the sun set, to live my life
long. I am the expression of Your love through all space
and time.

I carry You with me; I am Yours and You are mine.
Never have You deserted nor left me on my own,
not even in my most shameful hours of wrong.
Your knowledge is more than I can fathom.
I could love no other as You do me.

But still my spirit searched, through varying degrees of
unrest. I cried out in pain, screamed, demanded, and
confessed. I had abused myself and taken this life for granted.
Yet You did not forsake me, refused to turn Your back on
me, and I ask for Your forgiveness, I, your loving daughter,
now a woman.

You have shared with me so much, and You continue to
give. Because of You a blessed life I live.
This choice of free will, mine, to create who I was and who
I am. I have trust and faith in You, comprehending,
finally, only the good is true.

Conclusion

Conclusion

I dedicate this book to the universal consciousness, the infinite wisdom, the eternal presence known as God. This presence, which is glorified throughout every religion and race of man, has many names by which we praise Him for the creation of our magnificent world. This world that we've been given is a playground for the manifestation of our dreams which God lends to us so we too can be creators and momentarily glimpse existence through His eyes.

If it were not for the relationship I have developed with Source over the last several years, I would not have optimism in my heart, would not trust in the good that exists throughout mankind. To all who have awakened spiritually, I thank you and all those mentors and spiritual scholars who so graciously blazed the trail for myself and others.

In this process, despite my ups and downs, I have become more loving, empathetic, and thoughtful. I regret nothing, not a single step along the path, for I needed Life's complexities to formulate my life and journey.

What life is, I do not know for sure, except that it is what you make of it. On these pages, I have shared my perspectives and my personal struggles. I thank those of you who have chosen to read *Tales of the Human Condition*. I hope reading this book was as healing for you, as writing it was for me.

Please know you are never alone. Perhaps, sometimes, lonely, but never, ever alone.

Acknowledgements

Big thanks to . . .

Every person who supports me by buying this book. It is an incredible treasure to do what I love: write. I feel so blessed to have the means to have brought this book to life. This book has been a journey of will and determination six years in the making.

Those whom I have met through this process are now my extended family and permanent fixtures in my life.

Patrick Peterson, you encouraged me, believed in me as a writer, and gave so generously to me in order to make this book possible. I will never forget your love and support.

Margo Fitzsimmons, my mother, you are one of the reasons I write. I thank you.

Those who inspired these poems and are forever immortalized in words on these pages, you may or may not know who you are, but without you, I would have had no company on this journey of Life.

God, last but of course not least, is a fitting place to end, for in the end we all meet our Maker. I am so grateful and appreciative for the words and insights that You, Source, enable me to understand, present, and share with others, to articulate the all-encompassing challenges and triumphs of this human state. I thank you for unconditionally loving me, for I struggle still and am imperfect.

Biography

Millicent Ally's fondest early memories are of her mother, an aspiring novelist, reading to young Millie chapters from her own book. An avid reader, Ally's mother further influenced Ally with the gift of Robert Louis Stevenson's A Child's Garden of Verses. An only child, whose mother and stepfather moved the family from coast to coast and town to town, Ally found her truest companionship in poetry and books. And, at the age of thirteen, she found that the poetry she had been reading had taken root. It was then that Ally began to write, employing lyric and verse as therapy to deal with the challenging circumstances she faced.

From then until now, Ally has written because she is compelled to do so. Even so, for most of her life, Ally wrote only for herself and a few special friends. It wasn't until 2006, during the course of what she remembers as an emotionally difficult year, that the idea of sharing her poems more widely occurred to her, when a friend and spiritual advisor suggested Ally collect her poetry in a book. Encouraged by this, and by the support of a professor who exhibited interest in her writing, Ally began the journey which has found its fulfillment in this collection.

Still compelled to tell stories, Ally is currently attending the prestigious Writer's Boot Camp in Santa Monica, California, studying television and screen-writing.

www.ingramcontent.com/pod-product-compliance
Lightning Source LLC
Chambersburg PA
CBHW071721040426
42446CB00011B/2168